At world's end, begin

Jan Fortune

Cinnamon Press
:: small miracles from distinctive voices ::

Published by Cinnamon Press
www.cinnamonpress.com
The right of Jan Fortune to be identified as author of this work has been asserted by her in accordance with the Copyright, Designs and Patent Act, 1988. © 2023, Jan Fortune
ISBN 978-1-78864-137-1
British Library Cataloguing in Publication Data. A CIP record for this book can be obtained from the British Library.
All rights reserved. No part of this publication may be reproduced, stored in a retrieval system, or transmitted in any form or by any means, electronic, mechanical, photocopying, recording or otherwise without the prior written permission of the publishers. This book may not be lent, hired out, resold or otherwise disposed of by way of trade in any form of binding or cover other than that in which it is published, without the prior consent of the publishers.
Designed and typeset in Bodoni by Cinnamon Press.
Cover design by Adam Craig © Adam Craig.
Cinnamon Press is represented by Inpress

Author's Note

When I moved to Finistère, Brittany in late 2020 I read an article about the year in Japan being divided into 24 seasons or 'solar terms', with further subdivision into 72 micro-seasons, each lasting 3 to 5 days. Observing my new environment through micro-seasons seemed like an opportunity to become acquainted with the land I now dwell on (a garden surrounded by forest, full of indigenous wild plants, with a small orchard and a river running through it). So I wrote a haiku for each of the micro-seasons and interspersed these with eight slightly longer poems representing the Celtic wheel of the year with its quarter and cross-quarter days, four lunar and four solar, traditionally marking the year in the Celtic places of Ireland, Scotland, Wales, Cornwall and Brittany.

The collection's title is from 'Finistère' which means 'the end of the land/world', a name bequeathed by the Romans. In Breton the name is 'Penn-ar-Bed', which means both the 'end and head (or start) of the world'; most endings also being beginnings.

Author Biography

Jan Fortune was born in Middlesbrough, read theology at Cambridge and completed a doctorate in feminist theology at Exeter University. She has worked as a teacher, priest (ordained at the first ordination of women to the CofE) and charity director and is the founding editor of Cinnamon Press. She mentors writers across genres and hosts a writing community, Kith, that includes weekly prompts, courses and inspiration for the writing life at https://janfortune.com/

Her previous publications include non-fiction titles in alternative education and parenting; a book for writers: *Writing Down Deep: an alchemy of the writing life*; several novels, most recently *Saoirse's Crossing*, *The Casilda Trilogy* and *The Standing Ground Trilogy*, and several poetry collections, including *Slate Voices* (a collaborative collection with Mavis Gulliver) and *Stale Bread & Miracles*.

Jan studied aromatherapy with the Well School, is a yoga nidrā teacher with the Independent Yoga Nidrā Network and is training as a herbal practitioner with the Plant Medicine School in Ireland. She lives in a surviving area of ancient forest in Finistère, Brittany.

Acknowledgements

The refrain at the end of 'Imbolc' is based on T*he Song of Solomon* 2:11-12 and is referenced again at the end of 'April 3-7.' The refrain 'for the joy of the sweet green earth' at the end of 'Ostara' and referenced again at the end of 'Midsummer' was inscribed on the base of ceramic pieces made for me by the potter Peter Bolton, working in the 1970s-90s.

Contents

Imbolc	11
1: Rowan time—promise of spring	12
2: Rainwater days	13
3: Coming of spring	14
Ostara	15
4: Spring Equinox	16
5: Easter 2021	17
Beltaine	18
6: Yet more rain	19
7: Rains preparing for summer	20
8: Pentecost winds	21
9: Summer heat	22
Midsummer	23
10: Summer Solstice	24
11: Grey July	25
12: Lammas: greater heat	26
Lammas	27
13: Late summer	28
14: Beginning of autumn	29
15: Indian summer	30
Mabon	31
16: Autumn Equinox	32
17: Cold nights, morning mists	33
18: Greying to Samhain	34
Samhain	35
19: Turning to winter	36
20: Frost comes daily	37
21: Frost deepens	38
Winter Solstice:	39
22: Short days	40
23: Damp cold	41
24: Sharper cold	42

For Seth and Adam,
who've made this journey with me

At world's end, begin

Imbolc

Light comes slowly to Candlemass—
mares-milk pale, ewes bleating rhythms
of winter birth; life-scraps
of hope in ghosted sun,
scalpel leaves—snowdrop-thin—
pierce through earth, fisted
buds thawing ground
so recently wintered closed.

We shelter within—
kitchen a belly of scents,
birchwood flames,
comfort of poppyseed cake,
violet candles flickering chants—

winter will pass
rains will be gone,
flowers will bloom,
seasons of singing
will come.

1: Rowan time—promise of spring

February 2-6

First snowdrops appear.
Cow parsley crowds by the stream.
We turn towards hope.

February 7-11

Chaffinches arrive,
pinson des arbres singing,
change, change, all is change.

February 12-16

Thaw and freeze and thaw.
Geese in the snow, robin sits
on the post, turning.

2: Rainwater days

February 17-21

Grey clouds wash grey sky,
rain saturates, drenches soil
as we watch for flood.

February 22-26

Palest light fingers
daisy, primrose, celandine—
across banks, hearts strewn.

February 27-March 3

Moon waxing, near-full.
Morning frost on grass. Trees bud.
World yearning for light.

3: Coming of spring

March 4-8

When the geese are gone,
though morning mist turns to sun,
still a chill remains.

March 9-13

Wind owl-hoots through trees.
Rubicund hazel buds swell—
pregnant with what waits.

March 14-18

Woodpeckers at work.
Catkins shade the plastic urn
of ashes—remains.

Ostara

How she springs from the earth,
soft face of moss, shadow of tree—
verglas and vapour of haar
fizzing in sun, sudden and hot.

How she opens, lavender-washed,
rosemary-sharp with remembrance
of body, of blood, stone rolled away,
wants to be flowers, curls into nests.

How she rises hare-swift with delight,
petal, wind, cloud—*for the joy
of the sweet green earth.*

4: Spring Equinox

March 19-23

Willow soft with catkins.
Sleek magpies building a nest.
Two for Spring. For joy.

March 24-28

Morning frost returns.
In the high ash, first leaves bud.
One for sorrow, two...

March 29-April 2

Changeable weather,
distant thunder, shining sun,
still we're unsettled.

5: Easter 2021

April 3-7

Apple trees in leaf.
Great tits nest. Swallows return.
Season of singing.

April 8-12

Beneath the hedges,
violets, forget-me-nots.
Still, each morning: rime.

April 13-17

Blackthorn in blossom.
Talon-locked buzzards glide in
thermal courtship rites.

Beltaine

And come first season of flame,
we gather round fires,
fertile with losses to burn,
hopes seeding in ash,
yearning for change on the wind,
knowing there'll be more rain.

Earth beneath fire,
wind fanning flame,
water to flow with
green life again.

And come fire's rhythm and dance,
we look to the heart
of the flame, to the centre
around which we spin
desiring to spy the still point
that allows us, dizzy, to stand.

Earth beneath fire,
wind fanning flame,
water to flow with
green life again.

6: Yet more rain

April 18-22

Orchard blossoms pink.
Bees, fat with pollen, savour
warm days' nectar.

April 23-27

Swallows nest on roof.
Lone pike basks under bridge.
Full moon—planting seeds.

April 28-May 2

Yarrow in the grass,
silver-washed fritillary,
And the still pike hunts.

7: Rains preparing for summer

May 3-7

Dark moon in May rain,
banks of bluebells by the stream.
And yet we are cold.

May 8-12

Plantain tall with seed,
hawthorn heavy with flower,
scent of life and death.

May 13-18

Willow soft-furred,
showers turn to downpour, from
oil-curdled clouds—hail.

8: Pentecost winds

May 19-23

Hoar, rain, owl at night,
storms of dandelion seeds
searching for warm earth.

May 24-28

Wind on seedling herbs,
full blood-moon, turning sixty—
no tongues of flame,

May 29-June 3

Mugwort and sorrel,
stars of scarlet pimpernel,
foxgloves in heat, blaze.

9: Summer heat

June 4-8

Elder guards the gate.
Clouded Yellows flutter by—
resurrection heat.

June 9-13

Captive geese crying.
Oxeye daisies strew the grass.
Across sun—shadow.

June 14-18

Xanthic irises
cooling roots in the river.
Walk a narrow path.

Midsummer

for Ming

All day it rains. In the long grass,
only the oxeye daisies
open their eyes,
elder holds armfuls of blossom—foam
to bathe the wound of her peeled-away branch—

unashamed of her body's scars and age.
The forest leans in.
Though we see no sun this longest day,
we keep a vigil far into
the shortest night, long past

the bluest hour,
wake to light subdued by clouds,
grey humidity, elder bubbling
in sugared bowls,
champagne to wish you peace at the last—

in the joy
of the sweet green earth,
in the green space of the heart,
you rest.

10: Summer Solstice

June 19-24

Sudden summer cool.
Harvest of elderflowers—
soft wine for a death.

June 25-29

Yellow cinquefoil hedge,
seed pods of calendula
bow to summer rain.

June 30-July 4

Deer ticks in the field,
ladybirds and swallowtails,
Death's-head Hawk-moth squeals.

11: Grey July

July 5-9

Yarrow in flower.
Morning winds and changing skies—
humid July—grey.

July 10-14

We thin the fruit-set,
harvest white yarrow for tea—
work alongside bees.

July 15-20

Horehound Skippers tap
windows at night, self-heal sleeps,
wakes to clear blue sky.

12: Lammas: greater heat

July 21-26

She comes in day's heat—
Saturnia pyri, wings
beating between worlds.

July 27-31

Thunder. Rain torrents,
earth damp under sticky air—
Lammas-heat breaks.

August 1-5

Pentacled berries.
red on the rowan, protect
the quick and the dead.

Lammas

Somewhere there are grain harvests.
Here—elder heals her wounds,
puts on berries, as apples arch
their branches with freight,
flowers offer up seeds—
calendula, poppy, timothy, yarrow,
purple heather on verges,
everywhere scent of abundance,
gathering in—but, oh—this
more fragile place—
skin over bones,
blood, heart,
         stuttering
in summer storms—
drenched, cold—
         trying to fathom
how it continues to beat.

13: Late summer

August 6-10

Sky clouds late summer,
still apples green, ripening
as the winds blow cold.

August 11-15

Late summer sun burns
blue. Between humid showers,
kestrel scans for prey.

August 16-20

High yellow ragweed,
candy-clouds of thistle-down
tip towards autumn.

14: Beginning of autumn

August 21-25

Fine fast rain then sun,
nettle seeds for winter bread—
gathered at blue moon.

August 26-30

Sturgeon moon waning
to summer's end, cool wind's breath
softening sunset.

August 31-September 5

Soft late-summer sun
whispers of season turning.
Lizard runs through time.

15: Indian summer

September 6-10

Shot of nettle seeds,
crickets serenading dusk—
a dark moon crescents.

September 11-15

Small Copper female,
dead on the *grenier* floor.
First apples ripe.

September 16-20

As the weather turns,
full moon heralds Equinox,
winds slam windows shut.

Mabon

Here at the tipping point—
there was a marriage once,
in another country,
a girl I hardly recognise.
A boy I only thought
I knew. And, only a year ago,
a birth. A baby, held en route
to another life. How to balance
so much against the weight
of the world? I only know
that this giant moon
will not let me sleep tonight,
fills my restless heart
with her orange light, sings
the harvest home, calls me
by name to turn
towards winter, wounded,
blessed.

16: Autumn Equinox

September 21-25

First apples gathered.
Night-owl calls the harvest moon
to dazzle the stars.

September 26-30

High winds, squally rain,
black beetle in the attic
where water seeps in.

October 1-5

Moths infest the rug,
waning crescent beneath clouds
gathering their storm.

17: Cold nights, morning mists

October 6-10

Dark moon, swallows gone,
no geese return, river swells
as leaves, still green, fall.

October 11-15

First leaves turn yellow.
As we ward off cluster flies,
the river erupts.

October 16-20

Orchard's leaves falling,
though the forest remains green.
One apple still hangs.

18: Greying to Samhain

October 21-25

Babble of river,
footsteps sound along the path,
breeze rustles: listen.

October 26-30

Rain falls from blue sky,
ferns, rust and incarnadine,
one clover in bloom.

October 31-November 4

Tall ash losing leaves.
Larch, needles shimmering gold,
faces the winter.

Samhain

After this, darkness will gather,
cold wrap us round,
death sing her lullabies,
and if we listen—
we'll hear our names,
ask what it is
she needs us to learn, turn
to the dark, its loamy scent
enriching our dreams,
its caves inviting:
rest,
leave the seeds to germinate,
sit by the fire feeding the ancestors
stories, blood.

We will face
the silence—
dip our hands in its pool,
drink deep.

19: Turning to winter

November 5-9

Air-misted to ice,
overnight, the ash leaves fall,
ivy in full bloom.

November 10-14

In the holloway,
shadows of alder, birch, oak,
screen late autumn sun.

November 15-19

The night, orange-lit.
Bones of trees in silhouette.
On the full moon, blood.

20: Frost comes daily

November 20-24

Sky a sheet of ice,
high ash tree branches slipping
on pitiless frost.

November 25-29

Forest path a mulch,
stone rain clatters down by night,
gales keen morning cold.

November 30-December 4

Friends write of first snow.
Here, November moon stays bright
as ice as she wanes.

21: Frost deepens

December 5-9

Wind howling its grief
into rain, hail, silence.
Then the robin sings.

December 10-14

Ivy and holly,
mistletoe and moss, greening
this naked winter.

December 15-19

Grass sharpens its blades
on the frozen air—whetstone
of the knife-blue day.

Winter Solstice:

Although, for a sliver of time,
our held breath poised at autumn's Equinox,
that fragile balance teetered, slid
from the light, blinking, uncertain
of so much bounty, its blaze
guttering in unsteady increments
towards this longest night.

And even now, as we pause between
winter dark and the short day's orange dawn,
we wonder which way to turn
as we shelter in midwinter's grace,
contemplate its fallow depths, so still
the heart can be heard, welcome
the comfort of rest, ask if we have the courage

                              to face the light

22: Short days

December 20-24

In winter's hedgerow,
dock, nettle, a single stand
of broom—yellow light.

December 25-29

Brown leaves against mud,
only ivy bears berries
through the rain-drenched cold.

December 30-January 2

And as the year turns,
moss covers the fallen ash
and the moon is dark.

23: Damp cold

January 3-7

New moon thin as thought,
pale wash of sky as rain clears
to hint at cold light.

January 8-12

After rains, dawn fog
hangs in an inconstant sky
over trees, grieving.

January 13-17

Full moon lights the sky,
owl calling her thrill of death
as the river turns.

24: Sharper cold

January 18-22

Robin in the oak.
On the holloway, a doe
startles the winter.

January 23-27

Meadow a soft sponge,
hard bones of the pruned orchard
scratch the charcoal sky.

January 28-February 1

Waiting for Imbolc,
dawn creeps late through the poplars,
at world's end, begin.

Ingram Content Group UK Ltd.
Milton Keynes UK
UKHW011320190523
422025UK00018B/112